PEGASUS AND OTHER POEMS

By the same author

Translations

THE GEORGICS OF VIRGIL

THE AENEID OF VIRGIL

WITH CHARLES FENBY (EDITORS)
ANATOMY OF OXFORD

THE FRIENDLY TREE

OVERTURES TO DEATH

CHILD OF MISFORTUNE

STARTING POINT

POEMS IN WARTIME

WORD OVER ALL

THE POETIC IMAGE

POEMS 1943-1947

AN ITALIAN VISIT

COLLECTED POEMS 1954

PEGASUS

and Other Poems

by

C. DAY LEWIS

HARPER & BROTHERS
NEW YORK

PEGASUS AND OTHER POEMS

Printed in the United States of America

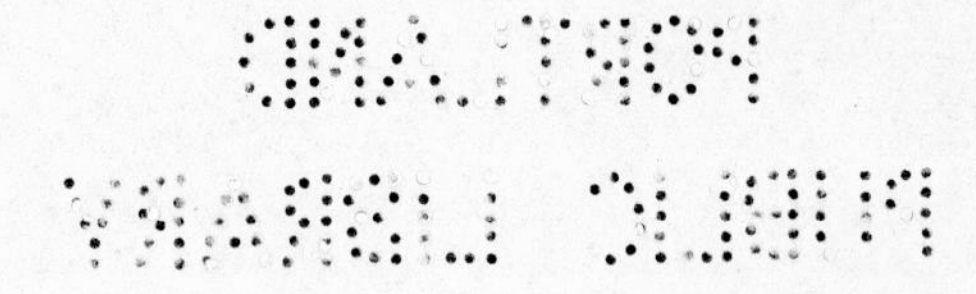

Library of Congress catalog card number: 58-5424

CONTENTS

Part One

Part Two

Part Three

To

JILL

PART ONE

Pegasus

(In Memoriam: L. B. L.)

It was there on the hillside, no tall traveller's story.
A cloud caught on a whin-bush, an airing of bleached
Linen, a swan, the cliff of a marble quarry –
It could have been any of these: but as he approached,
He saw that it was indeed what he had cause
Both to doubt and believe in – a horse, a winged white horse.

It filled the pasture with essence of solitude.
The wind tiptoed away like an interloper,
The sunlight there became a transparent hood
Estranging what it revealed; and the bold horse-coper,
The invincible hero, trudging up Helicon,
Knew he had never before been truly alone.

It stood there, solid as ivory, dreamy as smoke;
Or moved, and its hooves went dewdropping so lightly
That even the wild cyclamen were not broken:
But when those hooves struck rock, such was their might
They tapped a crystal vein which flowed into song
As it ran through thyme and grasses down-along.

'Pegasus,' he called, 'Pegasus' – with the surprise
Of one for the first time naming his naked lover.
The creature turned its lordly, incurious eyes
Upon the young man; but they seemed to pass him over
As something beneath their pride or beyond their ken.
It returned to cropping the violets and cyclamen.

Such meekness, indifference frightened him more than any
Rumoured Chimaera. He wavered, remembering how
This milk-white beast was born from the blood of uncanny
Medusa, the nightmare-eyed: and at once, although
Its brief glance had been mild, he felt a cringing
And pinched himself to make sure he was not changing

Into a stone. The animal tossed its head;
The white mane lifted and fell like an arrogant whinny.
'Horses are meant to be ridden,' the hero said,
'Wings or no wings, and men to mount them. Athene
'Ordered my mission, besides, and certainly you
'Must obey that goddess,' he cried, and flung the lassoo.

The cyclamen bow their heads, the cicadas pause.
The mountain shivers from flank to snowy top,
Shaking off eagles as a pastured horse
Shakes off a cloud of flies. The faint airs drop.
Pegasus, with a movement of light on water,
Shimmers aside, is elsewhere, mocking the halter.

So there began the contest. A young man
Challenging, coaxing, pursuing, always pursuing
The dream of those dewfall hooves: a horse which ran
Quicksilver from his touch, sliding and slewing
Away, then immobile a moment, derisively tame,
Almost as if it entered into a game.

He summoned up his youth, his conscious art
To tire or trick the beast, criss-crossing the meadow
With a web of patient moves, circling apart,
Nearing, and pouncing, but only upon its shadow.
What skill and passion weave the subtle net!
But Pegasus goes free, unmounted yet.

All day he tried for this radiant creature. The more he
Persevered, the less he thought of the task
For which he required it, and the ultimate glory.
So it let him draw close, closer – nearly to grasp
Its mane; but that instant it broke out wings like a spread
Of canvas, and sailed off easily overhead.

He cursed Pegasus then. Anger arose
With a new desire, as if it were some white girl
To stretch, mount, master, exhaust in shuddering throes.
The animal gave him a different look: it swirled
Towards him, circled him round in a dazzling mist,
And one light hoof just knocked upon his breast.

The pale sky yawns to its uttermost concave,
Flowers open their eyes, rivulets prance
Again, and over the mountainside a wave
Of sparkling air tumbles. Now from its trance
That holy ground is deeply sighing and stirring.
The heights take back their eagles, cicadas are whirring.

The furious art, the pursuer's rhythmic pace
Failed in him now. Another self had awoken,
Which knew – but felt no chagrin, no disgrace –
That he, not the winged horse, was being broken:
It was his lode, his lord, his appointed star,
He but its shadow and familiar.

So he lay down to sleep. Argos, Chimaera,
Athene in one solution were immersed.
Around him, on bush and blade, each dewdrop mirrored
A star, his riding star, his universe,
While on the moonlit flowers at his side
Pegasus grazed, palpable, undenied.

PEGASUS

A golden bridle came to him in sleep –
A mesh of immortal fire and sensual earth,
Pliant as love, compulsive as the sweep
Of light-years, brilliant as truth, perfect as death.
He dreamed a magic bridle, and next day
When he awoke, there to his hand it lay.

Wings furled, on printless feet through the dews of morn
Pegasus stepped, in majesty and submission,
Towards him. Mane of tempest, delicate mien,
It was all brides, all thoroughbreds, all pent passion.
Breathing flowers upon him, it arched a superb
Neck to receive the visionary curb.

Pegasus said, 'The bridle that you found
'In sleep, you yourself made. Your hard pursuit,
'Your game with me upon this hallowed ground
'Forged it, your failures tempered it. I am brute
'And angel. He alone, who taps the source
'Of both, can ride me. Bellerophon, I am yours.'

Psyche

He came to her that night, as every night,
Through the dark palace in a shape of darkness –
Or rather, it seemed to her, of light made invisible;
Came in a torrential swoop of feet
Or wings, and taking her filled her with sweetness:

Then slept, as the gods sleep who have no need
To dream. But she, awake in that dream palace
Where the wine poured itself and instruments played
At their own sweet will, began to feel afraid
That it was all some trick of the Love-Queen's malice.

A virgin once I roamed – my thoughts were vague
As a mother-of-pearl sky – before this beauty
Had grown to isolate me like a plague
From men, and set my sisters in jealous league.
It was I then who envied Aphrodite.

'Your husband,' they say, 'your husband is a dragon
'Sent to devour you.' And truly I am devoured
With love. But the daytimes drag, the tongues wag,
Distorting his unseen face; and I grow weak.
Can it be love that makes me such a coward?

Timidly then she touched his flank, which flowed
Like a river dreaming of rapids. Flesh it was,
Not scales. Each limb retraced was a midnight road
Humming with memories: each warm breath sighed
'Foolish girl, to believe only her eyes!'

Drowsing she closed her petals over this new
Delicate trust. But a quick remorse pierced her
That, doubting him, she had clouded her own love too;
And with it a seeming-pure desire to know
The facts of him who had so divinely possessed her.

Flesh of my flesh – yet between me and him
This maidenhead of dark. A voice, a stir,
A touch – no more, and yet my spirit's home.
Man, god, or fiend – blindly I worship him:
But he will tire of a blind worshipper.

'You must not look,' he said: but now I believe
Without seeing, what harm can it be to gaze?
He said, 'It is a secret.' Oh but in love
There are no secrets! and how can I ever prove
My love till I know what it is I might betray?

So ran the fatal argument; and so,
Closer than night, equivocal as a spy,
Into bed between them stole the lie . . .
She rose and lit her lamp. In the hall below
The harp strings broke, the wine jars all ran dry.

Heavy with sight, alarmed at new-born shadows,
She groped towards him. Night drew back in awe,
And the light became a clear, impassable window
Through which her love could gaze but never go.
The lamp burned brighter, inflamed by what it saw.

O moon-white brow and milky way of flesh!
Wings like a butterfly's on a warm stone
Trembling asleep! O rod and fount of passion,
Godlike in act, estranged in revelation! –
Once you were mine, were me, for me alone.

O naked light upon our marriage bed,
Let me touch you again and be consumed!
No reaching through the radiance you shed?
Breaking my faith, myself I have betrayed.
We that were one are two. Thus am I doomed.

She grasped her knife, but it refused the breast
She offered. Trying a finger on his arrows
She pricked herself, and love was dispossessed
By love of love, which means self-love. Unblest,
Unchecked – what a serpent flame letched at her marrow!

Darkness she craved now – but oblivion's pall
Not the true night of union. Anyway
The lamp would not blow out. Along the wall
A taloned shadow-beast began to crawl
Fawning and glum toward its naked prey.

A drop of burning oil upon his bare
Shoulder awoke him. Shuddering he beheld
Crusted over that face so innocent-fair,
The hangdog look, the dissolute anxious glare
Of lust, and knew his treasure had been spoiled.

So he passed from her, and at last she learnt
How blind she had been, how blank the world can be
When self-love breaks into that dark room meant
For love alone, and on the innocent
Their nakedness dawns, outraging mystery.

Followed the tasks – millet seed, poppy seed
And all. They keep her fingers busy, bind
A gaping heart. She tells the grain like beads:
Yet it is not her penance, it is her need
Moves mercy, proves and touches the Divine.

Dear souls, be told by me. I would not take
Love as a gift, and so I had to learn
In the cold school of absence, memory's ache,
The busy, barren world of mend and make,
That my god's love is given but never earned.

Baucis and Philemon

You see those trees on the hillside over the lake
Standing together – a lime tree and an oak –
With a stone circle around them? A strange thing
To find two trees wearing a marriage ring,
You say? You would not, if you knew their story. Yes,
They are wedded: the roots embrace, the leaves caress
One another still. You can hear them gossip together,
Murmuring commonplaces about the weather,
Rocked by gusts of memory, like the old.
In this evening light their wall is a hoop of gold. . . .

Philemon gazed into the cooling hearth,
And the hearth stared listlessly back at one whose fire
Was all but ash. His hands hung down like dry leaves
Motionless in a summer's aftermath –
Planter's hands, they could make anything grow.
So labourers sit at the end of a day or a lifetime.
The old man drowsed by the fire, feeling his death
Ripen within him, feeling his lifetime gone
Like a may-fly's day, and nothing to show for all
The works and days of his hands but a beaten path
Leading nowhere and soon to be overgrown.
Beside him, Baucis absently traced her memories
Which seemed a brood of children scattered long since
Among far lands; but always in him, her own –
Husband and child – where they began, they ended.
Knuckled like bark, palmed thin as a saint's relics,
Her hands rested from love. There was love in the shine
Of the copper pans, the thrift of a mended coverlet,
The scrubbed and sabbath face of the elm-wood table.
But now this wordless love, which could divine
Even in sleep his qualms and cares, awoke
And out of the speaking silence between them, heard

To dwindle down, to gutter and go out,

Consenting to the dark or jerking agonized
Shadows on the white faces round me!
The year goes out in a flash of chrysanthemum:
But we, who cell by cell and
Pang upon pang are dragged to execution,
Live out the full dishonour of the clay.
A bright bewildered April, a trance-eyed summer –
Mirage of immortality: then
The mildew mists, the numbing frosts, and we
Are rotting on the bough, who ripen to no end
But a maggot's appetite.
Where are my memories? Who has taken the memories
I stored against these winter nights, to keep me warm?
My past is under snow – seed-beds, bud-grafts,
Flowering blood, globed hours, all shrouded, erased:
There I lie, buried alive before my own eyes.
Are we not poor enough already
That the gods must take away? –

'Hush, my dear,'
Said Baucis, and laid her finger upon his lips
Like a holy wafer. 'We must not even dream
Ill of the gods. I too fear Death, but I fear
Him most because he will take one of us first
And leave the other alive. I fear his cruelty
Less than his charity.'
There was a knock at the door.
Her heart cried out – He has come for us both, bless him!
But it was only a couple of tramps or tinkers,
A bearded one and a younger, begging food,
All other doors in the village closed against them.
'You are welcome. It's nice to have company once in a while,'
She said to the grimy wayfarers, and strewed
Clean coverlets on the willow-wood couch for them
To rest while she blew up the fire again. Philemon
Brought out a well-smoked ham and his autumn fruit –

Radishes, endives, apples and plums, a honeycomb.
'You wandering folk see much of the world,' he said.
'Ah yes, there's nothing my father has not seen
In his time,' the young man answered: 'except perhaps
An eagle nesting with two turtle doves.'
The other smiled in his beard: his gaze, serene
As if it could weigh the gods and find them wanting,
Weighed now those hands like skeleton leaves, the bird-boned
Pair and the crumbs they shared, a copper pan
Gleaming, a rickety table freshened with mint.
All was amenity there, a calm sunshine
Of the heart. The young stranger, whose grey eyes
Were full of mischief and messages, winked at the elder:
'They could not treat us handsomer if we were gods.'
His companion nodded – at once the windless trees
In the orchard danced a fandango – and raised his cup
Of beechwood, charged to the brim with home-made wine:
'Philemon, a toast! I give you – your memories.'
He drained the cup; and when he had put it down,
It was still brimming. And in Philemon's soul
Welled up a miraculous spring, the wished release.

I am blind no longer. My joys have come home to me
Dancing in gipsy colours from oblivion.
Back on their boughs are the fruits of all my seasons
Rosy from sleep still, ripened to the core.
Look at the autumn trees content with their workaday
Russet and the grass rejoicing for mere greenness,
As the spring paths I trod through garden, through orchard,
Were content with violets. Oh chime and charm
Of remembered Junes, of killer frosts returning
To smile and be forgiven! Oh temperate haze
Maturing my yesterdays, promise of good morrows! –
Seventy years have I lived with Contentment,
And now for the first time I see her face.
Now I can thank the gods, who mercifully

Changed my despair into a cup full of blessings
And made a vision grow where a doubt was planted.

Baucis, weeping and smiling, knelt to adore
The elder god: who said, 'You had a wish too?'
With a glance at her husband's shadowless face, she replied,
'You have done one miracle. How could I ask more?
He is content. What more did I ever ask?'
'Nevertheless, an unspoken prayer shall be answered
When the prayer is good, and not to have voiced the prayer
Is better. Death shall not part you. Now follow me.'
They helped each other up the slow hillside
Like pilgrims, while the two gods went before.
When they looked back, their cottage in the combe below
Was changed – cob walls to pearl and thatch to gold –
A lodge for deity, almost as marvellous
As the wonder in their eyes. 'Ah, that is no
Miracle,' Hermes said, 'or if it is,
The miracle is yours.' Then Zeus affirmed, 'The seed
Hears not the harvest anthem. I only show you
A jewel your clay has formed, the immortal face
Of the good works and days of your own hands:
A shrine after my heart. Because I know you
Faithful in love to serve my hearth, my earth,
You shall stay here together when you go. . . .'

They climbed that hill each evening of their lives
Until, one day, their clasped hands uttered leaves
And the tired feet were taken underground.
'Goodbye, dear wife,' he called as the bark closed round,
And his branches upheld the cry in a carol of birds.
She yearned to his oaken heart, with her last words
Sweet as lime blossom whispering on the air –
'It's not goodbye.'
                    We found them growing there
And built the wall about them; not that they need
A ring to show their love, or ever did.

Ariadne on Naxos

(*A Dramatic Monologue*)

Between the hero's going and the god's coming
She paced a flinty shore, her windflower feet
Shredded and bleeding, but the flesh was numb
Or the mind too delirious to heed
Its whimpers. From the shore she vainly dredged
The deep horizon with a streaming eye,
And her strained ears like seashells only fetched
A pure pale blare of distance. Listlessly
She turned inland. Berries on bushes there
Watched her like feral eyes: she was alone:
The darkening thicket seemed a monster's fur,
And thorn trees writhed into a threat of horns.
She walks a knife-edge here, between the woe
Of what is gone and what will never go.

O many-mooded One, you with the bared
Horizons in your eye, death in your womb,
Who draw the mariner down to a choked bed
And write his name upon an empty tomb –
Strangle him! Flay the flesh from his dishonoured
Bones, and kiss out his eyes with limpets! – No,
Drown my words! Who is the faithless now? Those eyes
Were true, my love. Last night, beside the myrtle,
You said 'For ever', and I saw the stars
Over your head, and then the stars were lost in
The flare and deluge of my body's dawn.
False dawn. I awoke. Still dark. Your print upon me
Warm still. A wind, chilling my nakedness,
Lisped with the sound of oars. It was too dark
To see the wake of your bold, scuttling ship,
Or I'd have reeled you back on that white line,

As once . . . Is it because I saved you then
That you run from me as from a place accursed?
  What is it in the bushes frightens me so?
A hide for nothing human. Coalfire eyes
Penning me on the beach. You had a kingdom
In your eyes. When you looked at me with love,
Were you only seeing a way to it through me?
I am a girl, unversed in the logic of heroes –
But why bring me so far, rescuing me
From my father's rage, to leave me on this island
For the wild beasts? leave me like a forgotten
Parcel, or a piece of litter you had no time
To bury when you had used it under the myrtle?
Already a star shows. It is a day, an age
Since we came here. Oh, solitude's the place
Where time congeals and memories run wild.
  I put the ball of thread into your hands.
It is my own heartstrings I am paying out
As you go down the tunnel. I live with you
Through the whole echoing labyrinth, and die
At each blind corner. Now you have come back with
A bloody sword, a conqueror's tired smile.
For you, the accustomed victory: for me,
Exultation, miracle, consummation.
Embracing you, the steel between us, I took
That blood upon myself, sealing our bond
Irrevocably with a smear of blood,
Forgetting that a curse lifted falls elsewhere
And weighs the heavier, forgetting whose blood it was.
Did you hear my mother's willing, harsh outcry
Under the bull, last night? and shrink from your
Accomplice in the hot act, remembering
Whose daughter she is and whose unnatural son
She helped you butcher in the labyrinth?
  I was a royal child, delicately nurtured,
Not to be told what happened once a year

Beneath the mosaic floor, while the court musicians
Played louder and my father's face went still
As a bird listening for worms. But the maids gossiped;
And one day, when I was older, he explained –
Something about war crimes, lawful deterrents,
Just compensation for a proved atrocity.
It seemed nothing to do with flesh and blood,
The way he talked. Men have this knack for embalming
And burying outraged flesh in sleek abstractions.
Have you, too, found already a form of words
To legitimize the murdering of our love?
Ah well, I was not guiltless – never a thought for
The writhing give-and-take of those reparations
Until, with the last consignment of living meat
To be fed to the man-bull in the maze, you came.
    You with the lion look among that huddle
Of shivering whelps – I watched you from the gate-tower
And trembled, not in pity, but afraid
For my own world's foundations. When our hands
Touched at the State Reception, I knew myself
A traitor, wishing that world away, and found
My woman's heart – sly, timorous, dangerous creature,
Docile but to the regent of her blood,
Despising the complexities men build
To cage or to hush up the brute within.
What were parents and kingdom then? or that
Poor muzzled freak in the labyrinth, my brother?
– Forgotten all. Forgetfulness, they say,
Is the gods' timeliest blessing or heaviest curse.
A bundle of fear and shame, too much remembering,
I lie, alone, upon this haunted isle.
    A victim for a victim is the law.
Is there no champion strong enough to break
That iron succession? Listen! What is this word
The bushes are whispering to the offshore breeze?
'Forget'? No. Tell me again. 'Forgive.' A soft word.

I'll try it on my tongue. Forgive. Forgive. . .
How strangely it lightens a bedevilled heart!
Come out of the thorn thicket, you, my brother,
My brother's ghost! Forgive the clue, the sword!
Forgive my fear of you! Dead, piteous monster,
You did not will the hungry maze, the horns,
The slaughter of the innocents. Come, lay
Your muzzle on my forsaken breast, and let us
Comfort each other. There shall be no more blood,
No more blood. Our lonely isle expands
Into a legend where all can dream away
Their crimes and wounds, all victims learn from us
How to redeem the Will that made them so.

So on the dark shore, between death and birth,
Clasping a ghost for comfort, the girl slept.
Gently the night breeze bore across that firth
Her last, relinquishing sob: like tears unwept,
Windflowers trembled in the eye of night
Under the myrtle. Absence whirred no more
Within her dreamless head, no victim cried
Revenge, no brute fawned on its conqueror.
At dawn, far off, another promise broken,
The hero's black sail brought his father death.
But on that island a pale girl, awoken
By more than sunlight, drew her quick, first breath
Of immortality, seeing the god bend down
And offer a hoop of stars, her bridal crown.

PART TWO

A Riddle

What is this bird
Who purloins the gold from your teeth, the pearls from your lips
To star in its nest
With any old garish domestic scraps and strips?
Who thieves for its hoard
Like a jackdaw, but builds as trig and snug as the goldcrest?

Who stabs her own breast
To nurture the nestlings? who fetches them worms in his beak
Out of sweet lawn or carrion?
What is this anomalous creature at once unique
As the phoenix chaste,
Faithful as bullfinch, immoral and many as sparrows?

A starling for fun,
For sorrow a nightingale; the golden oriole
Seen through umbrageous
Thickets; the lark which a clear sky swallows up whole:
This manifold one
Flies higher than rocketing hope, sings best in a cage.

Seasonable Thoughts for Intellectuals

(*at Portland Bill*, 1949)

Cold chisels of wind, ice-age-edged,
Hammered hard at the marble block of
This mutilated island. Wind like a wedge
Splitting the cross-grained, bitter sea.
What a pity no artist or master mason
Aims the blows blind Nature lays on!

Flint flakes of a wintry sea
Shaling off the horizon
In endless, anonymous, regimental order.
Fish or fowl should laugh to see
Such penitential hordes of water.
Not so merrily laugh we.

A shag, wave-hopping in emblematic flight
Across that molten iron, seems
Less a bird than the shadow of some bird above,
So invulnerably it skims.
But there's no sun, and Neptune's unreflective,
And anyway, who wants a fowl's directive? . . .

O sea, with your wolverine running,
Your slavering over the land's end,
Great waves gulping in granite pot-holes,
Smacking your lips at the rocks you'd devour,
Belching and belly-rumbling in caves,
Sucking your teeth on the shingle! –
How sad to think that, before
You've more than nibbled a trillionth of the meal,
A piece of jelly which came from your maw
Many aeons ago, and contracted a soul,
May atomize earth and himself and you –
Yes, blow the whole bloody issue back into the blue.

The Committee

So the committee met again, and again
Nailed themselves to the never-much-altered agenda,
Making their points as to the manner born,
Hammering them home with the skill of long practice.

These men and women are certainly representative
Of every interest concerned. For example, A. wears
Integrity like a sheriff's badge, while B.
Can grind an axe on either side of a question:
C. happens to have the facts, D. a vocation
For interpreting facts to the greater glory of Dogma:
E. is pompously charming, diffidently earnest,
F. is the acid-drop, the self-patented catalyst.
Our chairman's a prince of procedure, in temporizing
Power a Proteus, and adept in seeming to follow
Where actually he leads – as indeed he must be,
Or the rest would have torn him to pieces a long time ago.
Yet all, in a curious way, are public-spirited,
Groping with their *ad hoc* decisions to find
The missing, presumed omnipotent, directive.

Idly the sun tracing upon their papers
Doodles of plane-leaf shadows and rubbing them out:
The buzz of flies, the gen of the breeze, the river
Endlessly stropping its tides against the embankment:
Seasons revolving with colours like stage armies,
Years going west along the one-way street –
All these they ignore, whose session or obsession
Must do with means, not ends. But who called this meeting
Of irreconcileables? Will they work out some positive
Policy, something more than a *modus vivendi*?
Or be adjourned, *sine die*, their task half done?

So the committee, as usual, reached a compromise –
If reach is the word, denoting, as it ought to,
A destination (though why should destiny not
Favour a compromise, which is only the marriage
For better or worse between two or more incompatibles,
Like any marriage of minds?) and left the table,
There being no further business for today.
And the silent secretary wrote up the minutes,
Putting the leaves in order. For what? the eye
Of higher authority? or the seal of the dust?
Or again, to be dispersed irreparably
When the hinge turns and a brusque new life blows in?
And I regret another afternoon wasted,
And wearily think there is something to be said
For the methods of the dictatorships – I who shall waste
Even the last drops of twilight in self-pity
That I should have to be chairman, secretary,
And all the committee, all the one-man committee.

The Wrong Road

There was no precise point at which to say
'I am on the wrong road'. So well he knew
Where he wanted to go, he had walked in a dream
Never dreaming he could lose his way.
Besides, for such travellers it's all but true
That up to a point any road will do
As well as another – so why not walk
Straight on? The trouble is, *after* this point
There's no turning back, not even a fork;
And you never can see that point until
After you have passed it. And when you know
For certain you are lost, there's nothing to do
But go on walking your road, although
You walk in a nightmare now, not a dream.

But are there no danger-signs? Couldn't he see
Something strange about the landscape to show
That he was near where he should not be?
Rather the opposite – perhaps the view
Gave him a too familiar look
And made him feel at home where he had no right
Of way. But when you have gone so far,
A landscape says less than it used to do
And nothing seems very strange. He might
Have noticed how, mile after mile, this road
Made easier walking – noticed a lack
Of grit and gradient; *there* was a clue.
Ah yes, if only he had listened to his feet!
But, as I told you, he walked in a dream.

You can argue it thus or thus: either the road
Changed gradually under his feet and became
A wrong road, or else it was he who changed
And put the road wrong. We'd hesitate to blame

THE WRONG ROAD

The traveller for a highway's going askew:
Yet possibly he and it become one
At a certain stage, like means and ends.
For this lost traveller, all depends
On how real the road is to him – not as a mode
Of advancement or exercise – rather, as grain
To timber, intrinsic-real.

He can but pursue
His course and believe that, granting the road
Was right at the start, it will see him through
Their errors and turn into the right road again.

The Pest

That was his youthful enemy, fouling the azure
With absolute mirk risen from god knows where –
A zero mood, action's and thought's erasure,
Impassable as rock, vapid as air.
When angels came, this imbecile thing infesting
His home retired to its sanctum below stairs;
But emerged, sooner or later, clammily testing
His hold on grace, his bond with the absent stars:
Till the horror became a need, the blacked-out sky
A promise that his angels would reappear,
A proof of light. Then the curse played its sly
Last trick – it thinned away, it was never there.
If it has gone for good, will he mope and die
Like a pauper with the lice washed out of his hair?

Almost Human

The man you know, assured and kind,
Wearing fame like an old tweed suit –
You would not think he has an incurable
Sickness upon his mind.

Finely that tongue, for the listening people,
Articulates love, enlivens clay;
While under his valued skin there crawls
An outlaw and a cripple.

Unenviable the renown he bears
When all's awry within? But a soul
Divinely sick may be immunized
From the scourge of common cares.

A woman weeps, a friend's betrayed,
Civilization plays with fire –
His grief or guilt is easily purged
In a rush of words to the head.

The newly dead, and their waxwork faces
With the look of things that could never have lived,
He'll use to prime his cold, strange heart
And prompt the immortal phrases.

Before you condemn this eminent freak
As an outrage upon mankind,
Reflect: something there is in him
That must for ever seek

To share the condition it glorifies,
To shed the skin that keeps it apart,
To bury its grace in a human bed –
And it walks on knives, on knives.

George Meredith, 1861

Whether it was or not his wish,
His real wish, he could never know:
But, after it happened, it seemed as if
A total stranger had struck the blow –
Some liberator out of the blue
Or hooded fanatic within himself.
The victim's cry for mercy came
Like a cry from his own heart, instantly gashed
By the knowledge of all he had aimed to undo.
So one they were, that severing blow
Could not but mortally hurt him too:
The deed came home to him in a flash
(Yet still too late), and at last he knew
The terrible meaning of 'one flesh'.

Historians now might take the view
That this was one more – though a crucial one –
Incident of his war within.
He'd been the battlefield long enough
As well as a combatant, when he withdrew
Scorching the earth behind him thus,
To whatever was left of integrity.
If they merely say that he saved his own skin,
They miss the point. Though he could not be
Occupied, utterly possessed again,
He has bought invulnerability
Too dear: such broad areas blackened, deadened –
How few of those sensitive threads remain
Which kept him in touch with hell, with heaven!

Betrayal is always a self-betrayal
Where love is concerned. The beautiful place,
Mortgaged by our ancestral sin,
Grows more untenable and more unreal

Each time, however needfully, we sell
Some share of it, buying with certain loss
Uncertain reprieve for our dwindling demesne . . .
So he, whose choice or necessity willed
The blackened earth, the liberating blow,
Is pent in the fruitless policies of brain.
While through his ghostly orchards tread
A murdered love and an unfulfilled
Agony, he walks elsewhere; and oh!
His silenced heart cannot tell him he is dead.

The Mirror

To make a clean sweep was the easiest part,
Though difficult enough. Anger of grief
Strengthened her hand and kept the silly heart
From dallying over his relics for relief.

To burn the letters, send back the keepsakes, wipe
His fingerprints off what little remained her own –
The girl stood over herself with a swift whip
And lashed until the outrageous task was done.

She had detached her flesh from his flesh, torn
It loose like a sea-anemone from a rock.
Now in that bare room where, lest he return,
All else was changed (she could not change the lock)

She took one careful invalid step, gauging
How much the ice of solitude would bear,
Then sat to her glass, as women do, assuaging
Chaotic thoughts with the clear, known image there.

No blood at the lips, no scars on the limpid brow,
Her face gazed out, vacant and undistracted,
A mere proscenium – nothing to show
For the tragedy, or farce, lately enacted.

True, it was not the first time nor the second
That love had lured her into a dead end.
She knew it all: but on this she had not reckoned –
The trick of a mirror upon the wall behind

Which cast in hers an endless, ever-diminished
Sequence of selves rejected and alone,
Cast back in her teeth the falsehood that she was finished
With love's calamities, having survived this one.

THE MIRROR

Seven devils, each worse than the one she had expelled,
Entering now that swept and garnished room,
Image on image on image in the glass she felt
Sucking her down into a vacuum,

A hell of narrowing circles. Time and again
Would she sit at the glass, helplessly reviling
The self that had linked her failures into a chain,
An ineluctable pattern. Love's too willing

Victim and love's unwilling poisoner, she
Would always kill the joys for which she died.
'Deep within you,' whispered the fiends, 'must be
'A double agent, false to either side. . . .'

Fallen at last, hurled beyond hope or terror,
Gathering doom about her, the girl now saw
Her hand, which had not strength to break the mirror,
Grope for the sleeping tablets in a drawer.

An Episode

So then he walled her up alive
(It seemed that her betrayal must deserve
What his own agony felt like – the slow choking
Of breath and pore in a close grave)
And waited. There was no cry from her, no knocking.

– Waited for pain to end, with her
Who had been his love and any comer's whore.
Soft-spoken dreams revealed how he was wanting
The victim to turn comforter –
A chastened ghost, an unreproachful haunting.

Presently the blank wall grew eyes
That hunted him from every covert ease
And thickset pain. He felt as if heart were searching
For heart. He saw in those whitewashed eyes
A look neither forgiving nor beseeching.

His bloody fingers tore at the wall,
Demolishing what could never salve nor seal
Its crime, but found in the nook where he had placed her
No twisted limbs, no trace at all.
His heart lay there – a mess of stone and plaster.

Love and Pity

Love without pity is a child's hand reaching,
A behemoth trampling, a naked bulb within
A room of delicate tones, a clown outraging
The heart beneath the ravished, ravisher skin.
Pity without love is the dry soul retching,
The strained, weak azure of a dog-day sky,
The rescuer plunging through some thick-mined region
Who cannot rescue and is not to die.
Pitiless love will mean a death of love –
An innocent act, almost a mercy-killing:
But loveless pity makes a ghost of love,
Petrifies with remorse each vein of feeling.
Love can breed pity. Pity, when love's gone,
Bleeds endlessly to no end – blood from stone.

A Meeting

Meeting the first time for many years,
What do they expect to see
Of the beings they made once, for better and worse,
Of each other – he and she?

A shrine to lost love? a hovel for guilt?
A vacant historic pile?
Something in ruins? something rebuilt
In a grand or a makeshift style?

Whatever is here to be freshly scanned,
Their view will be overcast:
Though they'll encounter, smile, shake hands,
They can only meet in the past –

Meet at the point where they parted, in
The house of what once they were,
Haunted by ghosts of what they might have been
Today, had they lived on there.

The life they had fashioned long ago
Seemed close as a honeycomb;
And if anything couples these strangers now
Who were each other's home,

It is grief that the pureness and plenitude of
Their love's long-flowering day
Could, like baser, flimsier stuff,
Corrupt or melt away.

Nothing left of the cells they stored
With joy, trust, charity
For years? . . . Nature, it seems, can afford
Such wastefulness: not we.

The Tourists

Arriving was their passion.
Into the new place out of the blue
Flying, sailing, driving –
How well these veteran tourists knew
Each fashion of arriving.

Leaving a place behind them,
There was no sense of loss: they fed
Upon the act of leaving –
So hot their hearts for the land ahead –
As a kind of pre-conceiving.

Arrival has stern laws, though,
Condemning men to lose their eyes
If they have treated travel
As a brief necessary disease,
A pause before arrival.

And merciless the fate is
Of him who leaves nothing behind,
No hostage, no reversion:
He travels on, not only blind
But a stateless person.

Fleeing from love and hate,
Pursuing change, consumed by motion,
Such arrivistes, unseeing,
Forfeit through endless self-evasion
The estate of simple being.

In Memory of Dylan Thomas

'it was Adam and maiden'

Too soon, it is all too soon
Laments our childhood's horn
Husky and cool at the close
Of its dove-note afternoon.
Too soon, a red fox echoes
Old on the hunted hill
Where dewfall mirrors the dawn
And dawn rides out for a kill.
It is too soon, too soon
Wails the unripened barley
To flailing storms: *too soon*
Pipes the last frail leaf in the valley.

A poet can seem to show
Animal, child and leaf
In the light of eternity, though
It is but the afterglow
From his consuming love,
The spill of a fabulous dawn
Where animal, leaf and child,
Timelessly conceived,
With time are reconciled.

Now we lament one
Who danced on a plume of words,
Sang with a fountain's panache,
Dazzled like slate roofs in sun
After rain, was flighty as birds
And alone as a mountain ash.
The ribald, inspired urchin
Leaning over the lip
Of his world, as over a rock pool
Or a lucky dip,

Found everything brilliant and virgin,
Like Adam who went to school
Only with God, and like Adam
He gave that world a tongue.
Already he has outsung
Our elegies, who always
Drew from creation's fathomless
Grief a pure drop of praise.

Edward Elgar

(1857–1934)

1

A boy among the reeds on Severn shore
Sound-bathing: a ghost humming his cello tune
Upon the Malvern hills: and in between,
Mostly enigma. Who shall read this score?

The stiff, shy, blinking man in a norfolk suit:
The martinet: the gentle-minded squire:
The piano-tuner's son from Worcestershire:
The Edwardian grandee: – how did they consort

In such luxuriant themes? Not privilege
Nor talent's cute, obsequious ear attuned
His soul to the striding rhythms, the unimpugned
Melancholy of a vulgar, vivid age.

Genius alone can move by singular ways
Yet home to the heart of all, the common chord;
Beat to its own time, timelessly make heard
A long-breathed statement or a hesitant phrase.

For me, beyond the marches of his pride,
Through the dark airs and rose-imperial themes,
A far West-country summer glares and glooms,
A boy calls from the reeds on Severn side.

2

Orchards are in it – the vale of Evesham blooming:
Rainshine of orchards blowing out of the past.
The sadness of remembering orchards that never bore,
Never for us bore fruit: year after year they fruited,

But all, all was premature –
We were not ripe to gather the full beauty.
And now when I hear 'orchards' I think of loss, recall
White tears of blossom streaming away downwind,
And wish the flower could have stayed to kiss the fruit it formed.
Oh, coolness at the core of early summers,
Woodwind haunting those green, expectant alleys,
Our blossom falling, falling.

Hills are in it – the Malverns, Bredon, Cotswold.
A meadowsweetness of high summer days:
Clovering bees, time-honeyed bells, the lark's top C.
Hills where each sound, like larksong, passes into light,
And light is music all but seen.
Dawn's silvery tone and evening's crimson adagio;
Noonday on the full strings of sunshine simmering, dreaming,
No past, no future, the pulse of time unnoticed:
Cloud-shadows sweeping in arpeggios up the hillsides;
Grey, muted light which, brooding on stone, tree, clover
And cornfield, makes their colours sing most clear –
All moods and themes of light.

And a river – call it the Severn – a flowing-awayness.
Bray of moonlight on water; brassy flamelets
Of marigold, buttercup, flag-iris in water-meadows;
Kingfishers, mayflies, mills, regattas: the ever-rolling
Controlled percussion of thunderous weirs.
Rivers are passionate gods: they flood, they drown,
Roar themselves hoarse, ripple to gaiety, lull the land
With slow movements of tender meditation.
And in it too, in his music, I hear the famous river –
Always and never the same, carrying far
Beyond our view, reach after noble reach –
That bears its sons away.

Elegiac Sonnet

To Noel Mewton-Wood

A fountain plays no more: those pure cascades
And diamond plumes now sleep within their source.
A breath, a mist of joy, the woodsong fades –
The trill, the transport of his April force.

How well these hands, rippling from mood to mood,
Figured a brooding or a brilliant phrase!
Music's dear child, how well he understood
His mother's heart – the fury and the grace!

Patient to bear the stern ordeal of art,
Keyed to her ideal strain, he found too hard
The simple exercise of human loss.

He took his grief away, and we are less.
Laurels enough he had. Lay on his heart
A flower he never knew – the rose called Peace.

Sheepdog Trials in Hyde Park

A shepherd stands at one end of the arena.
Five sheep are unpenned at the other. His dog runs out
In a curve to behind them, fetches them straight to the shepherd,
Then drives the flock round a triangular course
Through a couple of gates and back to his master: two
Must be sorted there from the flock, then all five penned.
Gathering, driving away, shedding and penning
Are the plain words for the miraculous game.

An abstract game. What can the sheepdog make of such
Simplified terrain? – no hills, dales, bogs, walls, tracks,
Only a quarter-mile plain of grass, dumb crowds
Like crowds on hoardings around it, and behind them
Traffic or mounds of lovers and children playing.
Well, the dog is no landscape-fancier: his whole concern
Is with his master's whistle, and of course
With the flock – sheep are sheep anywhere for him.

The sheep are the chanciest element. Why, for instance,
Go through this gate when there's on either side of it
No wall or hedge but huge and viable space?
Why not eat the grass instead of being pushed around it?
Like a blob of quicksilver on a tilting board
The flock erratically runs, dithers, breaks up,
Is reassembled: their ruling idea is the dog;
And behind the dog, though they know it not yet, is a shepherd.

The shepherd knows that time is of the essence
But haste calamitous. Between dog and sheep
There is always an ideal distance, a perfect angle;
But these are constantly varying, so the man
Should anticipate each move through the dog, his medium.
The shepherd is the brain behind the dog's brain,

But his control of dog, like dog's of sheep,
Is never absolute – that's the beauty of it.

For beautiful it is. The guided missiles,
The black-and-white angels follow each quirk and jink of
The evasive sheep, play grandmother's-steps behind them,
Freeze to the ground, or leap to head off a straggler
Almost before it knows that it wants to stray,
As if radar-controlled. But they are not machines –
You can feel them feeling mastery, doubt, chagrin:
Machines don't frolic when their job is done.

What's needfully done in the solitude of sheep-runs –
Those rough, real tasks become this stylised game,
A demonstration of intuitive wit
Kept natural by the saving grace of error.
To lift, to fetch, to drive, to shed, to pen
Are acts I recognise, with all they mean
Of shepherding the unruly, for a kind of
Controlled woolgathering is my work too.

Final Instructions

For sacrifice, there are certain principles –
Few, but essential.

I do not mean your ritual. This you have learnt –
The garland, the salt, a correct use of the knife,
And what to do with the blood:
Though it is worth reminding you that no two
Sacrifices ever turn out alike –
Not where this god is concerned.

The celebrant's approach may be summed up
In three words – patience, joy,
Disinterestedness. Remember, you do not sacrifice
For your own glory or peace of mind:
You are there to assist the clients and please the god.

It goes without saying
That only the best is good enough for the god.
But the best – I must emphasize it – even your best
Will by no means always be found acceptable.
Do not be discouraged:
Some lizard or passing cat may taste your sacrifice
And bless the god: it will not be entirely wasted.

But the crucial point is this:
You are called only to *make* the sacrifice:
Whether or no he enters into it
Is the god's affair; and whatever the handbooks say,
You can neither command his presence nor explain it –
All you can do is to make it possible.
If the sacrifice catches fire of its own accord
On the altar, well and good. But do not
Flatter yourself that discipline and devotion
Have wrought the miracle: they have only allowed it.

So luck is all I can wish you, or need wish you.
And every time you prepare to lay yourself
On the altar and offer again what you have to offer,
Remember, my son,
Those words – patience, joy, disinterestedness.

PART THREE

The House Where I Was Born

An elegant, shabby, white-washed house
With a slate roof. Two rows
Of tall sash windows. Below the porch, at the foot of
The steps, my father, posed
In his pony trap and round clerical hat.
This is all the photograph shows.

No one is left alive to tell me
In which of those rooms I was born,
Or what my mother could see, looking out one April
Morning, her agony done,
Or if there were pigeons to answer my cooings
From that tree to the left of the lawn.

Elegant house, how well you speak
For the one who fathered me there,
With your sanguine face, your moody provincial charm,
And that Anglo-Irish air
Of living beyond one's means to keep up
An era beyond repair.

Reticent house in the far Queen's County,
How much you leave unsaid.
Not a ghost of a hint appears at your placid windows
That she, so youthfully wed,
Who bore me, would move elsewhere very soon
And in four years be dead.

I know that we left you before my seedling
Memory could root and twine
Within you. Perhaps that is why so often I gaze
At your picture, and try to divine
Through it the buried treasure, the lost life –
Reclaim what was yours, and mine.

I put up the curtains for them again
And light a fire in their grate:
I bring the young father and mother to lean above me,
Ignorant, loving, complete:
I ask the questions I never could ask them
Until it was too late.

Father to Sons

That is the house you were born in. Around it
　A high old box-hedge inked out the view:
And this the garden it buxomly bounded,
　Where salvia, syringa, tobacco plants grew
　　Sheltered like you.

From snapshot to snapshot you can see yourselves growing
　And changing like figures on a dawn-struck frieze.
Ah, swift enough for my after-knowing
　That growth: but then you seemed to increase
　　By mere coral degrees.

So, to my fondness, you still may linger
　There at your romps and poker-faced ploys
Under the sweet pale downpour of syringa,
　Brief and sweet as all natural joys
　　In pathos and poise.

But you – what will you think of me, say of me,
　Turning these photographs over, years hence,
When I am dead? What shadow or ray of me
　Lingering for you then will cloud or enhance
　　Their brilliance?

Not the garden idyll, but a serpent mood it
　Concealed from the lens; not the innocent fall
Of light, but how I would often occlude it
　With guardian stance : is it this, above all,
　　That you must recall?

How often did words of mine, words out of season,
　Leave smouldering chagrin like fag-ends to char
Your fresh-painted sill of life! my unreason
　Or too much reason chill the air
　　For your tendril career!

If such bewilderments made your Eden
    A state you could not be sorry to slough,
Forgive. I still had much that even
    A god only gets at through mortal stuff
        To learn about love.

Son and Father

By the glim of a midwinterish early morning
Following habit's track over comatose fields,
A path of bleak reminder, I go to receive
The sacraments from my father, thirty years back.

Afterwards, walking home, unannealed, implacable,
I knew in the bones of my age this numb, flayed air,
These frozen grassblades rasping the foot, those hoar-drops
Which hung from a branch all day like unredeemed pledges.

Oh, black frost of my youth, recalcitrant time
When love's seed was benighted and gave no ear
To others' need, you were seasonable, you were
In nature: but were you as well my nature's blight?

That was thirty years back. The father is dead whose image
And superscription upon me I had to efface
Or myself be erased. Did I thus, denying him, grow
Quite dead to the Father's grace, the Son's redemption?

Ungenerous to him no more, but unregenerate,
Still on a frozen earth I stumble after
Each glimmer of God, although it lights up my lack,
And lift my maimed creations to beg rebirth.

Getting Warm – Getting Cold

(For Tamasin)

We hid it behind the yellow cushion.
'There's a present for you,' we called,
'Come in and look for it.' So she prowled
About the suddenly mysterious room –
'Getting warm,' she heard, 'getting cold.'

She moved in a dream of discovery, searching
Table and shelf and floor –
As if to prolong the dream, everywhere
But behind that cushion. Her invisible present
Was what she lived in there.

Would she never find it? Willing her on,
We cried, 'you're cold, you're warm,
You're burning hot,' and the little room
Was enlarged to a whole Ali Baba's cave
By her eyes' responsive flame.

May she keep this sense of the hidden thing,
The somewhere joy that enthralled her,
When she's uncountable presents older –
Small room left for marvels, and none to say
'You are warmer, now you are colder.'

Christmas Eve

Come out for a while and look from the outside in
At a room you know
As the firelight fitfully beats on the windowpane –
An old heart sinking low,
And the whispering melting kisses of the snow
Soothe time from your brow.

It is Christmastide. Does the festival promise as fairly
As ever to you? 'I feel
The numbness of one whose drifted years conceal
His original landmarks of good and ill.
For a heart weighed down by its own and the world's folly
This season has little appeal.'

But tomorrow is Christmas Day. Can it really mean
Nothing to you? 'It is hard
To see it as more than a time-worn, tinsel routine,
Or else a night incredibly starred,
Angels, oxen, a Babe – the recurrent dream
Of a Christmas card.'

You must try again. Say 'Christmas Eve'. Now, quick,
What do you see?
'I see in the firelit room a child is awake,
Mute with expectancy
For the berried day, the presents, the Christmas cake.
Is he mine? or me?'

He is you, and yours. Desiring for him tomorrow's
Feast – the crackers, the Tree, the piled
Presents – you lose your self in his yearning, and borrow
His eyes to behold
Your own young world again. Love's mystery is revealed
When the father becomes the child.

'Yet would it not make those carolling angels weep
To think how incarnate Love
Means such trivial joys to us children of unbelief?'
No. It's a miracle great enough
If through centuries, clouded and dingy, this Day can keep
Expectation alive.

The Newborn

(D. M. B.: April 29, 1957)

This mannikin who just now
Broke prison and stepped free
Into his own identity –
Hand, foot and brow
A finished work, a breathing miniature –
Was still, one night ago,
A hope, a dread, a mere shape we
Had lived with, only sure
Something would grow
Out of its coiled nine-month nonentity.

Heaved hither on quickening throes,
Tossed up on earth today,
He sprawls limp as a castaway
And nothing knows
Beside the warm sleep of his origin.
Soon lips and hands shall grope
To try the world; this speck of clay
And spirit shall begin
To feed on hope,
To learn how truth blows cold and loves betray.

Now like a blank sheet
His lineaments appear;
But there's invisible writing here
Which the day's heat
Will show: legends older than language, glum
Histories of the tribe,
Directives from his near and dear –
Charms, curses, rules of thumb –
He will transcribe
In his own blood to write upon an heir.

THE NEWBORN

This morsel of man I've held –
What potency it has,
Though strengthless still and naked as
A nut unshelled!
Every newborn seems a reviving seed
Or metaphor of the divine,
Charged with the huge, weak power of grass
To split rock. How we need
Any least sign
That our stone age can break, our winter pass!

Welcome to earth, my child!
Joybells of blossom swing,
Lambs and lovers have their fling,
The streets run wild
With April airs and rumours of the sun.
We time-worn folk renew
Ourselves at your enchanted spring,
As though mankind's begun
Again in you.
This is your birthday and our thanksgiving.

‘The Years O’

The days are drawing in,
A casual leaf falls.
They sag – the heroic walls;
Bloomless the wrinkled skin
Your firm delusions filled.
What once was all to build
Now you shall underpin.

The day has fewer hours,
The hours have less to show
For what you toil at now
Than when long life was yours
To cut and come again,
To ride on a loose rein –
A youth’s unbroken years.

Far back, through wastes of ennui
The child you were plods on,
Hero and simpleton
Of his own timeless story,
Yet sure that somewhere beyond
Mirage and shifting sand
A real self must be.

Is it a second childhood,
No wiser than the first,
That we so rage and thirst
For some unchangeable good?
Should not a wise man laugh
At desires that are only proof
Of slackening flesh and blood?

'THE YEARS O'

Faster though time will race
As the blood runs more slow,
Another force we know:
Fiercer through narrowing days
Leaps the impetuous jet,
And tossing a dancer's head
Taller it grows in grace.

Lot 96

Lot 96: a brass-rimmed ironwork fender.
It had stood guard for years, where it used to belong,
Over the hearth of a couple who loved tenderly.
Now it will go for a song.

Night upon winter night, as she gossiped with him
Or was silent, he watched the talkative firelight send
Its reflections twittering over that burnished rim
Like a language of world without end.

Death, which unclasped their hearts, dismantled all.
The world they made is as if it had never been true –
That firelit bubble of warmth, serene, magical,
Ageless in form and hue.

Now there stands, dulled in an auction room,
This iron thing – a far too durable irony,
Reflecting never a ghost of the lives that illumed it,
No hint of the sacred fire.

This lot was part of their precious bond, almost
A property of its meaning. Here, in the litter
Washed up by death, values are re-assessed
At a nod from the highest bidder.

Time to Go

The day they had to go
Was brilliant after rain. Persimmons glowed
In the garden behind the castle.
Upon its wall lizards immutably basked
Like vitrified remains
Of an archaic, molten summer. Bronze
Cherubs shook down the chestnuts
From trees over a jetty, where fishing nets
Were sunshine hung out in skeins
To dry, and the fishing boats in their little harbour
Lay breathing asleep. Far
And free, the sun was writing, rewriting ceaselessly
Hieroglyphs on the lake –
Copying a million, million times one sacred
Vanishing word, peace.
The globed hours bloomed. It was grape-harvest season,

And time to go. They turned and hurried away
With never a look behind,
As if they were sure perfection could only stay
Perfect now in the mind,
And a backward glance would tarnish or quite devalue
That innocent, golden scene.
Though their hearts shrank, as if not till now they knew
It was paradise where they had been,
They broke from the circle of bliss, the sunlit haven.
Was it for guilt they fled?
From enchantment? Or was it simply that they were driven
By the migrant's punctual need?
All these, but more – the demand felicity makes
For release from its own charmed sphere,
To be carried into the world of flaws and heartaches,
Reborn, though mortally, there.

TIME TO GO

So, then, they went, cherishing their brief vision.
One watcher smiled to see
Them go, and sheathed a flaming sword, his mission
A pure formality.

On a Dorset Upland

The floor of the high wood all smoking with bluebells,
Sap a-flare, wildfire weed, a here-and-gone wing,
Frecklings of sunlight and flickerings of shadowleaf –
How quick, how gustily kindles the spring,
Consumes our spring!

Tall is the forenoon of larks forever tingling:
A vapour trail, threading the blue, frays out
Slowly to a tasselled fringe; and from horizon
To horizon amble white eternities of cloud,
Sleepwalking cloud.

Here in this niche on the face of the May morning,
Fast between vale and sky, growth and decay,
Dream with the clouds, my love, throb to the awakened
Earth who has quickened a paradise from clay,
Sweet air and clay.

Now is a chink between two deaths, two eternities.
Seed here, root here, perennially cling!
Love me today and I shall live today always!
Blossom, my goldenmost, at-long-last spring,
My long, last spring!

View from an Upper Window

(For Kenneth and Jane Clark)

From where I am sitting, my windowframe
Offers a slate roof, four chimneypots,
One aerial, half of a leafless tree,
And sky the colour of dejection. I could
Move my chair; but, London being
What it is, all would look much the same
Except that I'd have the whole of that tree.
Well, window, what am I meant to do
With the prospect you force me to dwell upon – this tame
And far from original aperçu?

I might take the picture for what it can say
Of immediate relevance – its planes and tones,
Though uninspiring, significant because
Like history they happened to happen that way.
Aerial, chimneypots, tree, sky, roof
Outline a general truth about towns
And living together. It should be enough,
In a fluctuating universe, to see they are there
And, short of an atom bomb, likely to stay.
But who wants truth in such everyday wear?

Shall I, then, amplify the picture? track
The roof to its quarry, the tree to its roots,
The smoke just dawdling from that chimneystack
To the carboniferous age? Shall I lift those slates
And disclose a man dying, a woman agape
With love? Shall I protract my old tree heavenwards,
Or set these aerial antennae to grope
For music inaudible, unborn yet? But why,
If one's chasing the paradigm right forward and back,
Stop at embryo, roots, or sky?

VIEW FROM AN UPPER WINDOW

Perhaps I should think about the need for frames.
At least they can lend us a certain ability
For seeing a fragment as a kind of whole
Without spilling over into imbecility.
Each of them, though limited its choice, reclaims
Some terra firma from the chaos. Who knows? –
Each of *us* may be set here, simply to compose
From a few grains of universe a finite view,
By One who occasionally needs such frames
To look at his boundless creation through.

Dedham Vale, Easter 1954

for E. J. H.

It was much the same, no doubt,
When nature first laid down
These forms in his youthful heart.
Only the windmill is gone
Which made a miller's son
Attentive to the clouds.

This is the vale he knew –
Its games of sun and shower,
Willow and breeze, the truant
Here-and-there of the Stour;
And an immutable church tower
To polarize the view.

Yet, earnestly though we look
At such hard facts, the mill,
The lucid tower and the lock
Are something less than real.
For this was never the vale
He saw and showed unique –

A landscape of the heart,
Of passion nursed on calm,
Where cloud and stream drew out
His moods, and love became
A brush in his hand, and the elm tree
Lived like a stroke of art.

His sunburst inspiration
Made earthly forms so true
To life, so new to vision,
That now the actual view
Seems a mere phantom, through
Whose blur we glimpse creation.

DEDHAM VALE, EASTER 1954

It wears a golden fleece
Of light. However dull
The day, one only sees here
His fresh and flying colours –
A paradise vale where all is
Movement and all at peace.

The Gate

(For T. R.)

In the foreground, clots of cream-white flowers (meadowsweet?
Guelder? cow parsley?): a patch of green: then a gate
Dividing the green from a brown field; and beyond,
By steps of mustard and sanfoin-pink, the distance
Climbs right-handed away
Up to an olive hilltop and the sky.

The gate it is, dead centre, ghost-amethyst-hued,
Fastens the whole together like a brooch.
It is all arranged, all there, for the gate's sake
Or for what may come through the gate. But those white
flowers,
Craning their necks, putting their heads together,
Like a crowd that holds itself back from surging forward,
Have their own point of balance – poised, it seems,
On the airy brink of whatever it is they await.

And I, gazing over their heads from outside the picture,
Question what we are waiting for: not summer –
Summer is here in charlock, grass and sanfoin.
A human event? – but there's no path to the gate,
Nor does it look as if it was meant to open.
The ghost of one who often came this way
When there was a path? I do not know. But I think,
If I could go deep into the heart of the picture

From the flowers' point of view, all I would ask is
Not that the gate should open, but that it should
Stay there, holding the coloured folds together.
We expect nothing (the flowers might add), we only
Await: this pure awaiting –
It is the kind of worship we are taught.

The Great Magicians

To fish for pearls in Lethe,
Wash gold from age-long grief;
To give infinity a frame,
The may-fly a reprieve:

In a calm phrase to utter
The wild and wandering sky;
To reconcile a lover's Eden
With a madman's sty:

To mediate between
The candle and the moth;
To plug time's dripping wound, or spin
A web across hell's mouth:

Such feats the great magicians
Found within their powers,
Whose quick illusions bodied out
A world more whole than ours.

But the hollow in the breast
Where a God should be –
This is the fault they may not
Absolve nor remedy.

Moods of Love

1

The melting poles, the tongues that play at lightning,
All that gross hurricane hatched from a sigh –
These are the climax to his sure routine.
But first, a glance coins gold in the air, doves issue
From clasped hands, knots no one saw tied are tightening;
The card you chose, or were made to, wondrously
Turns up here there and anywhere like a djinn,
And borrowed time vanishes to amaze you.

Admire the 'fluence of this conjuring
As once again he runs the gamut through
Of tricks you can neither fathom nor resist,
Though well you know the old Illusionist
Employs for his whole repertoire only two
Simple properties – a rod, a ring.

2

Think of his transformations; thirsty babe,
Secret companion, devil, confidante,
Lapdog and sphinx – each hides that king whose orb
Is the whole earth grasped in a bare 'I want'.
Redder the rose for him, sadder the fall,
Who swells a trivial word into a portent,
Turns dust to diamond, shows the bantam tall,
The giant weak: nevertheless, most potent
When he comes back insidious and subdued
As an old jailbird begging one more chance.
Whether you trust him then, or look askance,
Or slam your door, at least don't act the prude:
He's what you've made of him: plausible, lewd
Or tough, he's your flesh – was a pure child once.

3

'Oh shelter me from the invisible rain
Corrodes my flesh piecemeal! Oh take me in –
I'll be your god, your man, your mannikin!'
Cry the gaunt lecher and the ignorant swain.

Dipped in eternity now, they find nowhere
A flaw in the magic circle of their embracing:
Two are reborn as one: where all is passing
They dream a now for ever and set fair.

Reborn! The very word is like a bell.
From the warm trance, the virgin arms awoken,
Each turns to his sole self. Out of the shell
They step, unchanged. Only a spell is broken.

Though there's no cure, no making whole, no fusion,
Live while you can the merciful illusion.

4

See, at a turn of her wrist, paradise open;
Dote, lover, upon a turquoise vein;
Feel how the blood flowers and the nerves go lilting
Like butterflies through an immortal blue.
This is creation morning. What could happen
But miracles here? The god you entertain,
The pure legend you breathe, no desert silting
Over your garden ever makes untrue.

New-seen, first-named, your own to hurt and heal,
This commonplace of skin, bone, habit, sense
Is now a place that never was before.
Lose and possess yourself therein: adore
The ideal clay, the carnal innocence.
Where all's miraculous, all is most real.

5

Inert, blanched, naked, at the gale's last gasp
Out of their drowning bliss flung high and dry
Above the undertow, the breakers' rasp,
With shells and weed and shining wrack they lie.
Or, as an isle asleep with its reflection
Upon the absolute calm, each answers each
In the twin trance of an unflawed affection
That shows the substance clear, the dream in reach.
By one arched, hollowing, toppling wave uptossed
Together on the gentle dunes, they know
A world more lucid for lust's afterglow,
Where, fondly separate, blind passion fused
To a reflective glass, each holds in trust
The other's peace, and finds his real self so.

6

The dance, the plumage, all that flaunting day
Of blood's clairvoyance and enchanter's wit
Making trite things unique – you reckon it
Tells more than brute necessity at play?

Unwise. Another tedious, piteous woman
Was Helen, got by heart. Can you adore
The human animal's ecstacy, yet ignore
The ground and primitive logic of being human? –

Deplore that closest viewed is clearliest changing,
And least enduring is the most enthralling?
That love breeds habit, habit brings estranging?
That highest flown means most abysmal falling?

When the flushed hour goes down, what residue
From its broad-glittering flood remains to you?

7

Shells, weed, discoloured wrack – a spring tide's litter
Dully recalling its lost element,
And one you live with, quarrelsome or complying,
Are all that's left of Aphrodite's birth.
Gone is the power she gave you to delight her,
The period of grace, so quickly spent,
When the day's walk was a white dream of flying,
Earth a far cry, she a sufficient earth.

Whether long use has now choked your desire
With its own clinker, or, abruptly parted
At love's high noon, incredulous you have stood
Suffering her absence like a loss of blood
Week after week, still, by the god deserted,
You worship relics of a sacred fire.

8

Beware! Such idolizing can divorce
Body and mind: the foam-bright fiction drains
Purpose away and sings you from your course.
Better a brutal twitching of the reins
And off, than this devouring pious whore
Who in a soft regret will twine you fast
Where thigh-bones mope along the tainted shore
And crazed beachcombers pick over their past.
Love is the venturing on: think – as you fare
Among strange islands, each a phantasy
Of home, giving your strength to what must be
Found and new-found through doubt, mirage, despair –
Weaving, unweaving her true self somewhere
Deep in your heart grows a Penelope.

9

If love means exploration – the divine
Growth of a new discoverer first conceived
In flesh, only the stranger can be loved:
Familiar loving grooves its own decline.

If change alone is true – the ever-shifting
Base of each real or illusive show,
Inconstancy's a law: the you that now
Loves her, to otherness is blindly drifting.

But chance and fretting time and your love change her
Subtly from year to year, from known to new:
So she will always be the elusive stranger,
If you can hold her present self in view.

Find here, in constant change, faithful perceiving,
The paradox and mode of all true loving.

Last Words

Suppose, they asked,
You are on your death-bed (this is just the game
For a man of words),
With what definitive sentence will you sum
And end your being? . . . Last words: but which of me
Shall utter them?

– The child, who in London's infinite, intimate darkness
Out of time's reach,
Heard nightly an engine whistle, remote and pure
As a call from the edge
Of nothing, and soon in the music of departure
Had perfect pitch?

– The romantic youth
For whom horizons were the daily round,
Near things unbiddable and inane as dreams,
Till he had learned
Through his hoodwinked orbit of clay what Eldorados
Lie close to hand?

– Or the ageing man, seeing his lifelong travel
And toil scaled down
To a flimsy web
Stranded on two dark boughs, dissolving soon,
And only the vanishing dew makes visible now
Its haunted span?

Let this man say,
Blest be the dew that graced my homespun web.
Let this youth say,
Prairies bow to the treadmill: do not weep.
Let this child say,
I hear the night bird, I can go to sleep.